Budget Basics

Pi Luna Press

ISBN: 978-0998686028

Pi Luna Press
Santa Fe, New Mexico
www.pilunapress.com

First Edition

Table of Contents

Introduction

Each of us has our own unique financial needs. Luckily, the process of making a budget applies to everyone. In this book, you'll create a budget for a fictitious character to learn about the process. Then you'll be prompted to create your own budget.

Budgets = Universal Tool

People = Unique Financial Needs

Meet Penny

Penny struggles with money because her income is inconsistent. When she earns more money, she spends more. When she earns less money, she struggles to pay her bills. She has over-drafted her bank account several times—and had to pay hefty fees. She's ready to make a change.

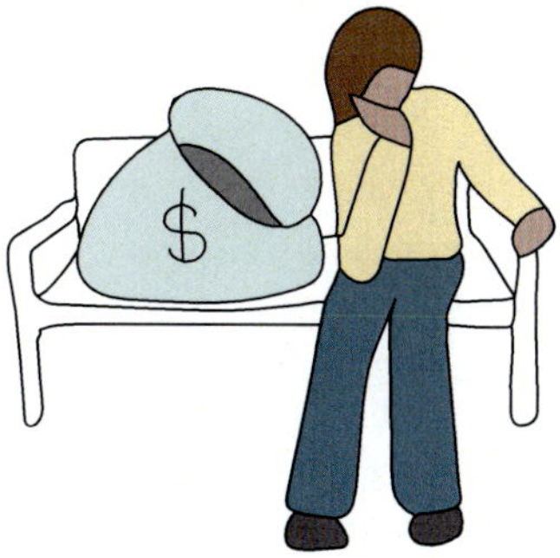

Inconsistent Income

The first part of a budget is income. Penny has a full-time administrative job at a school nine months out of the year, and also sells her artwork at art shows. When Penny sells her art, she does well and can earn over a thousand dollars in one night. Most months out of the year, however, she doesn't sell any paintings. Her income is inconsistent, making it difficult to manage. *Note: Since taxes is a topic beyond the scope this book, assume all income is after taxes. Visit www.pilunapress.com to learn about future books on taxes.*

Administrative Job

Penny earns $2,500 per month for 9 months out of the year.

Art Shows

Penny has 4 shows per year and earns on average $1,500 per show.

Average Monthly Income

One way Penny can work with her inconsistent income is to calculate the average monthly income over the course of a year. The average will help her make a budget and manage her finances.

Add all of the income amounts for the entire year and divide by the number of months.

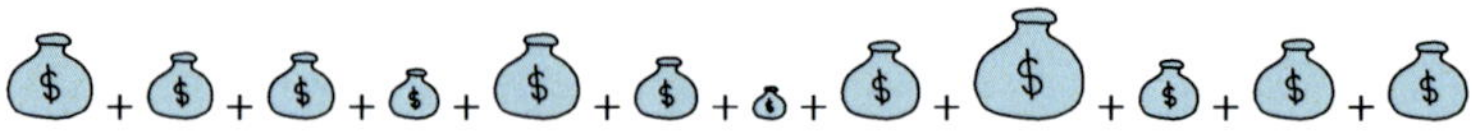

12 months

Exercise 1

1. Calculate Penny's average monthly income if she earns $2,500 per month for nine months at her administrative job and does four art shows, earning $1,500 at each. *Assume her earnings are after taxes.*

**See page 42 to check your answers.*

Determining Your Earnings

To determine your own average monthly income, you can use your previous year's earnings as an estimate. Most banks provide data on your deposits. If you have online banking, you can download your account activity. You can also look through your bank statements. Talk with someone at your bank to learn more about their services.

Working with the Average Monthly Income

Penny's average monthly income will become her monthly budget. She can use a savings account to keep her income stable each month.

Earning More

When Penny earns more than her average monthly income, she can place the extra amount into a savings account.

Earning Less

When she earns less, she can withdraw what she needs from her savings account.

Exercise 2

1. In May, Penny will earn $4,000. How much should she put in her savings account in order to maintain her average monthly income?

2. In June, Penny will earn $1,500. How much will she need to withdraw from her savings account to maintain her average monthly income?

Introduction to Spreadsheets

Budgets are living documents and need to change as your life changes. Creating a budget by hand makes it hard to revise later. Spreadsheets make it much easier. They can organize the information in a budget and perform calculations. Here, you'll learn how to make a budget in a spreadsheet. *You can use Microsoft Excel®, Google Sheets®, Numbers for Mac®, or Apache Open Office®.*

New to Spreadsheets?

If you've never used a spreadsheet application or want to go deeper into the topics covered here, check out *Spreadsheet Nuts & Bolts* by Pi Luna. Available at www.pilunapress.com.

- Print ISBN: 978-0998686004
- Ebook ISBN: 978-0998686042

Parts of a Spreadsheet

Columns

Columns are run vertically and are labeled with letters.

	A	B	C	D
1				
2				
3				

Rows

Rows run horizontally and are labeled with numbers.

	A	B	C	D
1				
2				
3				

Cell Names

A cell is a box. A cell's name is the column letter followed by the row number.

	A	B	C	D
1				
2				
3		B3		

Exercise 3

1. What is the name of the selected cell below?

	A	B	C	D
1				
2				
3				

Budgeting Income

The first part of a budget is income. Let's start by creating Penny's budget by entering her average monthly income.

Step 1

Open a blank spreadsheet. In the first cell, type, "Penny's Monthly Budget."

	A	B	C	D
1	Penny's Monthly Budget			
2				

Step 2

Press enter or return to complete the entry.

Step 3

Notice that the text is too long to fit in the cell. You can adjust the cell width to create more room. Start by placing your cursor on the column border at the top between A and B.

	A	B	C	D
1	Penny's Monthly Budget			
2				

Step 4

Click, hold and drag until the cell is wide enough.

	A		B	C
1	Penny's Monthly Budget			
2				

Step 5

Release the mouse and the column width will adjust.

	A	B	C
1	Penny's Monthly Budget		
2			

Step 6

Click to select the cell beneath "Penny's Monthly Budget."

	A	B	C
1	Penny's Monthly Budget		
2			

Step 7

Type "Income."

	A	B	C
1	Penny's Monthly Budget		
2	Income		

Step 8

Click on the cell to the right.

	A	B	C
1	Penny's Monthly Budget		
2	Income		

Step 9

Type Penny's average monthly income.

	A	B	C
1	Penny's Monthly Budget		
2	Income	$2,375	

Creating a Savings Plan

There are many ways to save money. One way is to transfer a percentage of your income each month to a separate savings account. Penny plans to save 15% of her income.

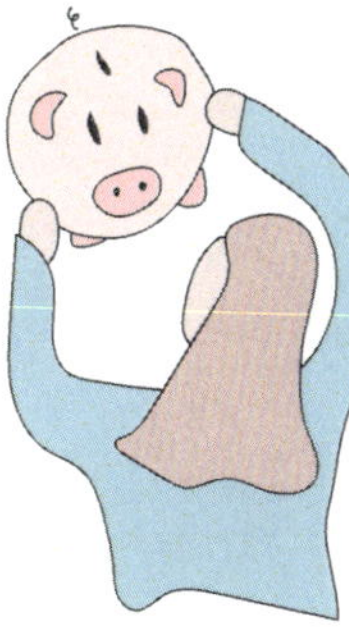

Exercise 4

1. If Penny saves 15% of her income each month and her average monthly income is $2,375, how much money will she save on average per month?

2. If Penny's continues to save that much every month, how much will she save in 5 years?

Spreadsheet Formulas

Spreadsheets do the math for you. To create a formula in your spreadsheet, first type an equal sign (=) and then type the formula.

Budgeting Savings

Let's continue creating Penny's budget by inserting a formula to calculate her savings.

Step 1

Open the spreadsheet you created. Click on the cell beneath "Income" and type "Savings."

	A	B	C
1	Penny's Monthly Budget		
2	Income	$2,375	
3	Savings		

Step 2

Click on the cell to the right and type an equal sign (=) to begin a formula.

	A	B	C
1	Penny's Monthly Budget		
2	Income	$2,375	
3	Savings	=	

Step 3

Since the amount of savings is based on the income, click on the income cell. It will become highlighted and its cell name, B2, will appear in your formula.

	A	B	C
1	Penny's Monthly Budget		
2	Income	$2,375	
3	Savings	=B2	

Step 4

Multiply (*) by the percentage of savings. *Note: To get the multiplication symbol, hold down the* (shift) *key and press the* (*8) *key on your keyboard. Now type 15%.*

	A	B	C
1	Penny's Monthly Budget		
2	Income	$2,375	
3	Savings	=B2*15%	

Step 5

Press (enter) and the amount of savings will be displayed.

	A	B	C
1	Penny's Monthly Budget		
2	Income	$2,375	
3	Savings	$356	

Managing Expenses

The third part of a budget is managing expenses. Penny needs to know the amount of each expense and how often it occurs so she can budget accordingly.

Types of Expenses

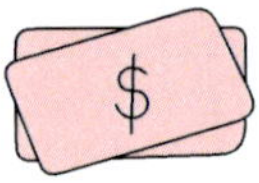

Amount

The amount of a single expense.

Frequency

How often the expense occurs.

Prorated Monthly Expense

The average monthly cost based on the amount and frequency of the expense.

Common Frequencies

Annually
1 time per year

Quarterly
4 times per year

Weekly
52 times per year

Semiannually
2 times per year

Monthly
12 times per year

Daily
365 times per year

Discussion

What are some examples of expenses for each of the frequencies above?

How Much Does Penny's Car Cost?

One expense that benefits from prorating is the cost of owning a car. You need to consider many different expenses: car payments, gas, oil changes, regular maintenance, registration, and insurance. These expenses happen at different times throughout the year. Prorating Penny's car expenses will help her be better prepared.

Exercise 5

1. Complete the table below with Penny's car-related expenses:

Expense	*Cost*	*Frequency*	*Annual Cost*
Car Payment	$195	Monthly	
Insurance	$376	Semiannually	
Registration	$52	Annually	
Car Washes	$10	Quarterly	
Oil Changes	$45	Quarterly	
Gas	$24	Weekly	

2. How much does Penny spend each year on her car?

3. What is Penny's prorated monthly car expense?

Needs & Wants: Finding the Balance

You can think about expenses as either needs or wants. Penny can decide which expenses are needs and which are wants to help her manage her spending.

Exercise 6

Decide which of the following expenses are needs and which are wants.

Expense	Need	Want
1. Rent/Mortgage	✓	
2. Car Expenses		
3. Health Insurance		
4. Internet Access		
5. Clothes		
6. Netflix		
7. Dining Out		
8. Gym Membership		
9. Pet Food		
10. Smartphone		
11. Retirement Savings		
12. Art Supplies		

The Price of Daily Coffee

Penny goes to a coffee shop everyday. One cup of coffee is not a huge expense, but her daily coffee purchases end up costing her more than she realizes.

Exercise 7

1. If Penny spends $4.95 for coffee every day, how much does that cost her for one year? *Use 365 for the number of days in the year.*

2. If she makes her own coffee, she'll need to buy 2 bags of beans each month. If each bag costs $9.95, how much would it cost her to make her own coffee everyday for a year?

3. In one year, how much would she save by making her own coffee instead of buying it from a coffee shop?

Penny's Dilemma

Penny can save money by making her own coffee, but there are some drawbacks. Coffee shops are convenient; they can be a great place to socialize, study, or read.

Middle Path

Eliminating every non-essential expense can feel like deprivation. Being too strict with herself puts Penny at risk of giving up on her budget. Creating a middle path will make her goals more achievable.

Exercise 8

1. Penny has decided to buy coffee at the coffee shop only on the weekends. If she buys a $4.95 cup twice a week, how much will she spend in a year? *There are 52 weeks in a year.*

2. What is the difference in price between going to the coffee shop everyday and going only on weekends?

Useful Life of Products

Another consideration in making a budget is the useful life of a product. Products eventually wear out or break down. Often lower priced products don't last as long as their higher-priced counterparts. The balance between initial cost and long-term value is a classic trade-off. Sometimes it's better to pay more up-front for a product that will last longer than to go with a cheaper product you'll have to replace sooner.

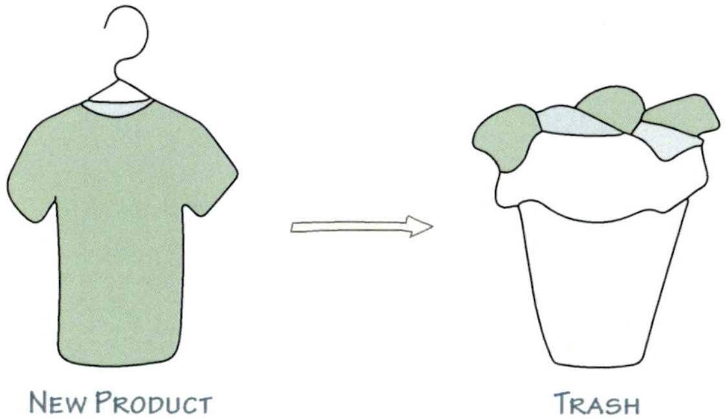

Comparing Ink Cartridges

Printer ink can be a regular expense. Many ink cartridges come with different pricing options. Regular ink cartridges cost less, but high-yield ink cartridges last longer. Let's compare 2 different options.

Regular Ink

A regular pack of black and color ink costs $39.99 and will print 160 pages.

High-Yield Ink

A high-yield pack costs $59.99 and will print 400 pages.

Exercise 9

1. Penny prints 800 pages per year. If she only bought regular ink cartridges, how much would she spend in one year?

2. If she bought high-yield ink cartridges, how much would she spend in one year?

Comparing Savings

When comparing the price of products, consider both the short-term benefit and the long-term benefit.

Short-Term Savings

Or

Long-Term Savings

Discussion

Do you think it is better to pay more up-front for a product with a longer useful life, or to pay less up-front for a product with a shorter useful life?

Budgeting Expenses

Let's enter Penny's expenses into her budget.

Step 1

Open your spreadsheet and enter Penny's expenses, such as those shown below. *Note: Most people have more expenses. For the sake of simplicity, Penny only has six expenses.*

	A	B	C
1	Penny's Monthly Budget		
2	Income	$2,375	
3	Savings	$356	
4	Rent	$950	
5	Utilities	$99	
6	Groceries	$250	
7	Eating Out	$175	
8	Car	$385	
9	Entertainment	$100	

Step 2

Under the last expense, type "Total Expenses."

	A	B	C
9	Entertainment	$100	
10	Total Expenses		

Step 3

Spreadsheets can add the values in a number of cells. Start by typing an equal sign [=], then "sum." Then open a set of parentheses [(].

	A	B	C
9	Entertainment	$100	
10	Total Expenses	=sum(	

Step 4

Click on the savings, which is the first expense, hold and drag to the entertainment expense. The name of the first cell, B3, and last cell, B9, will appear in your formula. Close the parentheses).

	A	B	C
1	Penny's Monthly Budget		
2	Income	$2,375	
3	Savings	$356	
4	Rent	$950	
5	Utilities	$99	
6	Groceries	$250	
7	Eating Out	$175	
8	Car	$385	
9	Entertainment	$100	
10	Total Expenses	=sum(B3:B9)	

Step 5

Press enter and the "sum" function will add the expenses.

	A	B	C
9	Entertainment	$100	
10	Total Expenses	$2,315	

Step 6

Under the "Total Expenses" cell, type, "Ending Balance."

	A	B	C
9	Total Expenses	$2,315	
10	Ending Balance		

STEP 7

Select the cell next to the right. Type an equal sign (=) to begin a formula.

	A	B	C
9	Total Expenses	$2,315	
10	Ending Balance	=	

STEP 8

Click on the amount of income. Its cell name, B2, will appear in your formula.

	A	B	C
1	Penny's Monthly Budget		
2	Income	$2,375	
3	Savings	$356	
4	Rent	$950	
5	Utilities	$99	
6	Groceries	$250	
7	Eating Out	$175	
8	Car	$385	
9	Entertainment	$100	
10	Total Expenses	$2,315	
11	Ending Balance	=B2	

Step 9

Press the subtraction (−) key on your keyboard and then click on the total expenses in cell B10.

	A	B	C
1	Penny's Monthly Budget		
2	Income	$2,375	
3	Savings	$356	
4	Rent	$950	
5	Utilities	$99	
6	Groceries	$250	
7	Eating Out	$175	
8	Car	$385	
9	Entertainment	$100	
10	Total Expenses	$2,315	
11	Ending Balance	=B2-B10	

Step 10

Press (enter) and the ending balance will be displayed.

	A	B	C
10	Total Expenses	$2,315	
11	Ending Balance	$60	

Unexpected Expenses

Sometimes you face unexpected car maintenance, house repairs, and medical bills. Paying for them can be a challenge. Penny just had an unpleasant surprise:

Credit Cards

Credit cards are easy to get and can be very convenient. But they come with risks. If you're not careful, you can end up in a nasty debt cycle.

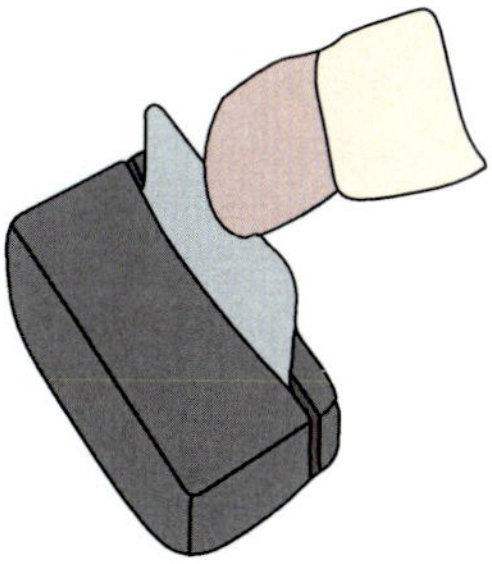

The Minimum Payment

Credit card companies will require a minimum payment each month.

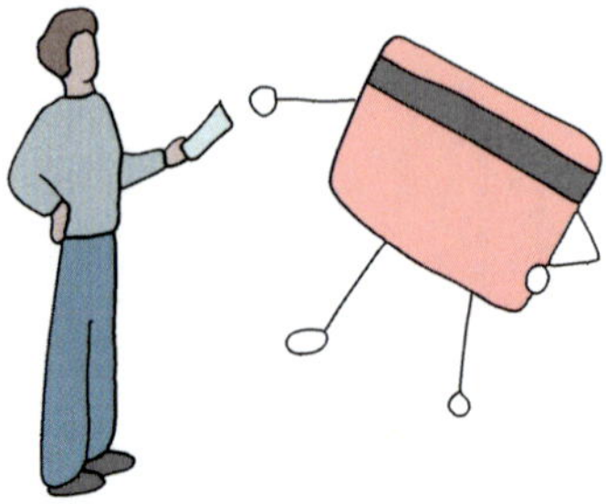

Calculating the Minimum Payment

Each credit card company calculates the minimum payment differently. A common way is to base it on a percentage of the balance. The balance includes your credit card purchases, plus interest, minus what you've already paid back.

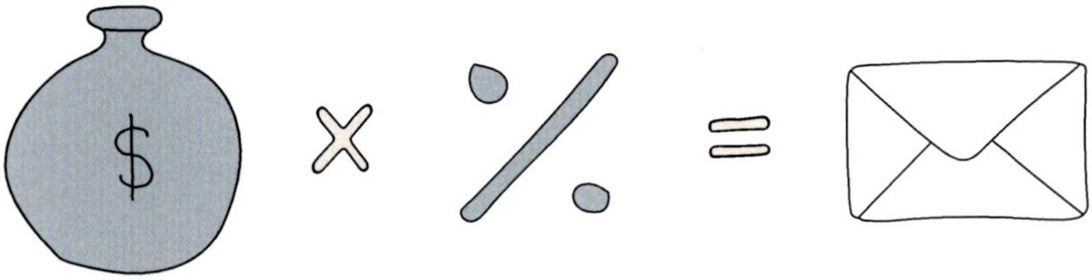

Multiply the balance *by the minimum percentage* *to calculate the minimum payment.*

Exercise 10

1. The minimum payment on Penny's credit card is 2% of the balance. If she owes $1,200, what is her minimum payment?

Budgeting Credit Cards

Once you've created a spreadsheet, you can easily add or delete expenses. Let's insert a new expense for Penny's credit card payment.

Step 1

Open your spreadsheet and right-click on the row number of the rent expense. *Note: If you're using a Mac, press* ctrl *on your keyboard while clicking on the row number.*

	A	B	C
1	Penny's Monthly Budget		
2	Income	$2,375	
3	Savings	$356	
4	Rent	$950	
5	Utilities	$99	

Step 2

A menu will appear. Click on "Insert."

	A	B	C
1	Penny's Monthly Budget		
2	Income	$2,375	
3	Savings	$356	
4	Delete	$950	
5	Insert	$99	
	Clear		

Step 3

A blank row will be inserted. Enter the new expense.

	A	B	C
1	Penny's Monthly Budget		
2	Income	$2,375	
3	Savings	$356	
4	Credit Card	$24	
5	Rent	$950	

Result

The spreadsheet automatically recalculates the total expenses and ending balance.

	A	B	C
11	Total Expenses	$2,339	
12	Ending Balance	$36	

Credit Card Interest

If you don't pay off your entire balance when the credit card payment is due, the bank will charge you interest. The greater your balance, the more interest you have to pay.

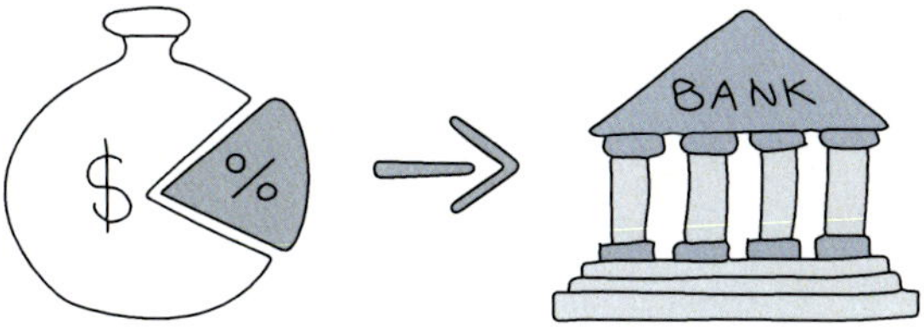

Rate per Month

The annual percentage rate (APR) is the percentage for one year. Since you will be required to pay credit card interest monthly, the APR needs to be divided by 12 to obtain the monthly interest rate.

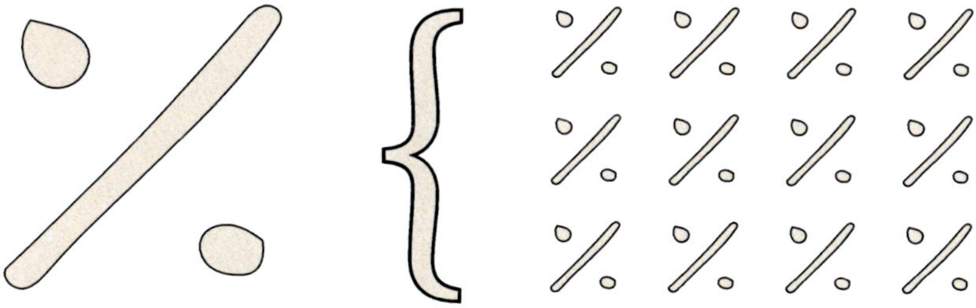

The Annual Percentage Rate (APR)

is divided by 12 to obtain the rate per month.

Exercise 11

1. Penny's APR is 18%. What is her rate per month?

Calculating Interest

Multiply the balance by the rate per month to calculate the interest the bank is charging you.

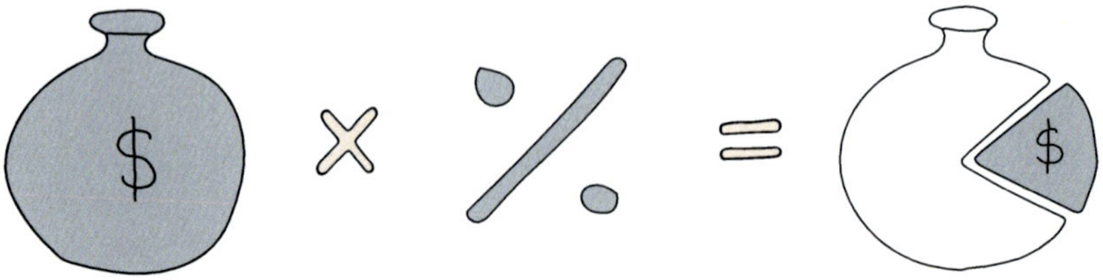

Multiply the balance *by the rate per month* *to calculate the interest.*

Exercise 12

1. Penny's balance is $1,200 and her APR is 18%. How much interest will she owe in her first month of credit card repayment?

Understanding Credit Card Interest

Each credit card payment is split into two parts. The first part goes to pay the interest and the second part goes to pay the balance.

Exercise 13

1. If Penny's minimum payment is $24 and her interest is $18, how much of her payment goes toward her balance?

2. Penny paid for her $1,200 car repair with her credit card. After her first payment of $24, how much does she still owe?

Paying More Than the Minimum

Penny can pay more than the minimum. Right now her budget is pretty tight and she doesn't have enough money to make a larger payment. She will need to reduce another area of her budget.

She could save a smaller percentage of her income.

Or she could reduce her eating out and entertainment budget.

Discussion

If you were Penny, how much would you pay on the credit card and how would you adjust your budget to accommodate the change?

Revising the Budget

Let's revise Penny's budget. Assume she will reduce her percentage of savings to 10% and increase her credit card payment to $200 per month. She will also decrease her eating out budget to $50 and increase her groceries budget to $300.

Step 1

Open your spreadsheet and double-click on the amount of savings.

	A	B	C
1	Penny's Monthly Budget		
2	Income	$2,375	
3	Savings	$356	

Step 2

The formula used to calculate the savings will appear. Change the percentage to 10%.

	A	B	C
1	Penny's Monthly Budget		
2	Income	$2,375	
3	Savings	=B2*10%	

Step 3

Press enter and the amount of savings recalculates.

	A	B	C
1	Penny's Monthly Budget		
2	Income	$2,375	
3	Savings	$238	

STEP 4

Change the groceries to $300, the eating out budget to $50, and the credit card to $200. Press enter.

	A	B	C
1	Penny's Monthly Budget		
2	Income	$2,375	
3	Savings	$238	
4	Credit Card	$200	
5	Rent	$950	
6	Utilities	$99	
7	Groceries	$300	
8	Eating Out	$50	
9	Car	$385	
10	Entertainment	$100	

RESULT

The total expenses and ending balance values recalculate accordingly.

	A	B	C
11	Total Expenses	$2,322	
12	Ending Balance	$54	

Projected Vs. Actual

Life happens, and sometimes you spend more than you planned to. After you make your budget, you have to keep track of your spending and see if you stayed within your budget and what, if any, changes you need to make.

Projected

The income you expected to earn and the expenses you expect to pay.

Actual

Your actual income and expenses may not match the budget you created.

Collecting Actual Amounts

Your bank statements will show a list of your expenses each month. You can use these statements to calculate your actual spending in each category. If you have online banking, you can also find this information in your account summary. Some banks will sort your expenses into categories for you. Speak with someone at the bank to learn more.

Budgeting Actual Amounts

At the end of the month, Penny can enter her actual income and expenses into her budget to see how well she stuck to her plan. She can make adjustments as needed in future months. Let's enter Penny's actual amounts into her budget.

Step 1

Open the spreadsheet, in Column C, and enter the actual amounts next to each category.

	A	B	C
1	Penny's Monthly Budget		
2	Income	$2,375	$2,375
3	Savings	$238	$238
4	Credit Card	$200	$200
5	Rent	$950	$950
6	Utilities	$99	$97
7	Groceries	$300	$288
8	Eating Out	$50	$84
9	Car	$385	$369
10	Entertainment	$100	$122

Step 2

You can copy the formulas used for the totals. Click on the "Total Expenses," hold, and drag down to the "Ending Balance" to select both cells.

	A	B	C
11	Total Expenses	$2,322	
12	Ending Balance	$54	

Step 3

Place your cursor on the bottom-right corner of the selection.

	A	B	C
11	Total Expenses	$2,322	
12	Ending Balance	$54	

Step 4

Click, hold and drag to the right.

	A	B	C
11	Total Expenses	$2,322	
12	Ending Balance	$54	

Step 5

Release the mouse button, and you'll see Penny's actual values in Column C.

	A	B	C
10	Total Expenses	$2,322	$2,348
11	Ending Balance	$54	$27

Discussion

In which areas did Penny overspend and in which did she spend less than expected?

Using Different Bank Accounts

Penny often goes over budget. One way she can manage her spending is to use different bank accounts.

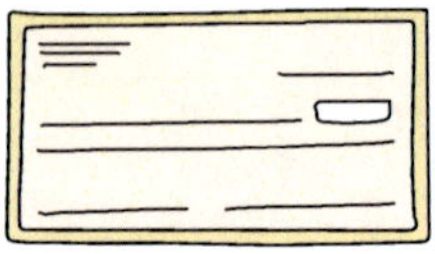

Debit/Checking

Her debit/checking account will be used for day-to-day purchases, such as coffee shops and eating out.

Savings

Her savings account will be used for her monthly savings. By putting the money in a separate account, she will be less likely to spend it.

Bills

She can have a bank account exclusively for bills and sign up for auto-pay to ensure those expenses always get paid on time.

Discussion

What are some other ways Penny can manage her spending habits?

Creating Your Own Budget

Now that you have explored Penny's budget, it's time to create your own. Use the following template to fill in your income, expenses and savings plan.

Income

Source of Income	*Amount*
Total Income	

Savings

Savings Plan	*Amount*
Total Savings	

Expenses

Type of Expense	*Amount*
Total Expenses	

Ending Balance

Ending Balance	

Answer Key

Exercise 1

1. $2,375

Exercise 2

1. $1,625
2. $875

Exercise 3

1. C2

Exercise 4

1. $356.25
2. $21,375

Exercise 5

1. $4,623
2. $385
3. $2,340
4. $752
5. $52
6. $38
7. $180
8. $1,261

Exercise 6

1. Answers will vary.

Exercise 7

1. $1,806.75
2. $238.80
3. $1,567.95

Exercise 8

1. $514.80
2. $1,291.95

Exercise 9

1. $199.95
2. $119.98

Exercise 10

1. $24

Exercise 11

1. 1.5%

Exercise 12

1. $18

Exercise 13

1. $6
2. $1,194

About the Author

Award-winning author Pi Luna integrates multiple learning styles to merge logic with meaning. As an artist, designer, and math instructor, Pi believes the best learning happens when both sides of the brain are engaged. She

is a nationally certified tutor (CRLA III) and has over 12 years experience tutoring and teaching math at the high school and college levels. Pi has a master's degree in Interdisciplinary Art from Goddard College, where she studied the connection between math, art, and psychology. To learn more, visit www.pilunapress.com.

Life Savings: Navigate the Financial Course

Winner of the best parenting and family issues book in the New Mexico/Arizona Book Awards, *Life Savings: Navigate the Financial Course* integrates math, art, and storytelling to bring personal finances to life. Meaningful examples delve deeply into some of life's most pivotal financial choices. Life Savings emphasizes critical thinking, spreadsheet proficiency, and note-taking skills, with custom artwork that invites you to learn in a structured, supported way.
ISBN: 978-0692438893

Spreadsheet Nuts & Bolts

If you run a business, work in an office, are a student, or want to manage your personal finances, learning how to use a spreadsheet will make your life easier. This book demystifies the process with step-by-step instructions, colorful illustrations, and practical tools.
ISBN: 978-0998686004

Made in United States
Orlando, FL
08 November 2026

90367947R00029